How to Analyze People

Proven Methods to Successfully Analyze Anyone

utter responsibility of the recipient reader. Under no circumstances will any legal responsibility or blame be held against the publisher for any reparation, damages, or monetary loss due to the information herein, either directly or indirectly.

Respective authors own all copyrights not held by the publisher.

The information herein is offered for informational purposes solely, and is universal as so. The presentation of the information is without contract or any type of guarantee assurance.

The trademarks that are used are without any consent, and the publication of the trademark is without permission or backing by the trademark owner. All trademarks and brands within this book are for clarifying purposes only and are the owned by the owners themselves, not affiliated with this document.

Table of Contents

Introduction

Congratulations on downloading this book, *"How to Analyze People: Proven Methods to Successfully Analyze Anyone"*.

I wrote this book with one intention: to teach you, and show you just how easy and effective it is to analyze ANYONE, no matter what your level of experience is, or who the person is. Now I'm no psychologist, but I can tell you that I've been using these methods throughout my whole adult life, and I tell you now in full confidence that what I am about to reveal to you has enhanced my success not just in my personal life, but my professional life too, and it WILL help you too if you apply the methods correctly.

Show me your friends, and I will tell you the kind of person you are. We all know this pretty well. We know that if we surround ourselves with the right people, we will ultimately be able to go far in life. Think about it. With the right company, you can be sure that you will have all the fun you want, enjoy every moment with other people, and be sure about someone's loyalty and a lot more. Unfortunately, while you may have all the right motives and a genuine heart, the truth is that you may be all alone. Other people may have different expectations from your interactions.

Obviously, this will mean that you cannot achieve whatever it is you wanted because when you all have different viewpoints about an issue, this mismatch makes it hard for you to succeed in whatever it is you are doing. That's where you need to learn how to analyze people to know them inside out. To understand those around you easily and know what people you should include in your friend's circle, you need to know how to analyze people effectively.

Analyzing people entails reading the different cues and elements attached to their personality. When you analyze someone, you look at the different aspects of their outward personality to find out different things about their inner personality and nature. This means you will be studying the way they talk, their body language, the things they talk about, how they dress up and various other factors.

If you aren't good at analyzing people, but want to develop this skill, then this book WILL help you accomplish that goal. Read on to find out how you can use my proven methods to give you success in analyzing anyone!

Analyzing people doesn't stop there. If you are able to analyze what people are thinking, then they may equally be able to read you like a book. Thus, the more you learn about body language and the way in which it works, the more likely you are to be able to make the best of your own body language and increase your chances of making friends and influencing people.

Communication is a two way thing, so you can be sure that just as you are observing others, they will be using the same set of values to judge who you are. That means that you will be able to present yourself in situations that would otherwise give you discomfort and know that the image that you are projecting is exactly the one that fits the occasion.

This will help you throughout your life to project a positive image that will get you further than an image that is not honed or worked on to any degree. You may think that accepting you at face value is enough, but when you have read this book, you will find out that others may be seeing you as something other than who you are – simply because you are not abiding by the rules of presentation yourself and may be coming over to others in a way that you do not wish.

Use the observations in the book to read others, but remember that they also apply to the way that people read you and with this information, you can improve the image that you project to others and fulfill your full potential in the workplace, in relationships and in your contact with other people.

Improving your body language, your presentation and the way that you approach things will enhance your life no end. You will also learn how to use your intuitive skills to the best of your ability, thus recognizing things that are not obvious to everyone else, but which prove to be right. That puts you in the driving seat and helps you considerably with your ability to read others and to let them see that part of you that you wish to show them, rather than the side of you that you may have been displaying unwittingly in the past. Win friends and influence people by learning what it takes to read others and applying this to your own life and it's a win-win situation.

Thanks again for downloading my book, I hope you enjoy it!

Chapter 1

Basics of Analyzing People

Understanding the psychology of different people helps you know the meaning associated with the different actions they take, which in turn helps you understand people better. Before starting with the techniques you need to use to analyze people, it is important to give you a little insight into the basics of profiling people.

1. People are Like Onions

Just like an onion has four major layers, a person too has four intrinsic layers that you need to understand in order to profile them. The deeper you pierce through these layers, the better you will be able to read and understand a person. The basic four layers are shown below but you do need to remember that these have exceptions and that you may miss vital signs and signals if you do not use these in conjunction with other clues that we have presented further on in the book:

✓ *Their Skin*

The first layer of a person is their skin. It doesn't tell you much about a person, but does reveal some aspects of their personality. For instance, the expressions on their face and their body language are cues that give you certain hints about their personality. Are they comfortable in the skin they are in? You can tell a lot about a person from what you see on the outside and it may be more apparent than you think. Body language is a powerful aid and we have gone into this in more detail in a future chapter.

✓ *Second Layer*

Once you get to know a person a little better and have had about three to four meetings with them, you get to know them a little deeper and can peek through their second layer. This layer reveals their likes, dislikes, interests, and preferences. For instance, you know your colleagues or classmates better than a stranger you met on the bus station because you have insight into the second layer of your classmates. This second layer is fairly easy to reach through the power of conversation and the more direct your line of discussion, the easier it is to discern what type of person it is that you are communicating with.

✓ *Third Layer*

The third layer of a person reveals a great deal of information about his or her personality and you get to find it out when you enter into a strong relationship with someone. For instance, you know your best friends, partner, and siblings much better than your colleagues. This side of a character is often hidden from those who do not know them well but you may just touch on it occasionally and notice by their reaction that you may have accidentally hit on a subject that is close to their heart. When you do, be careful how you approach the topic until you learn why this particular line of discussion caused the discomfort.

✓ *Fourth or Core Layer*

The core is the deepest layer of a person and holds information about a person that they hardly reveal to anyone. This simply means that getting to know the core of someone is quite a challenging task. This is the part of the person that is private. If you imagine the thought processes that go on in the mind of the individual, there is bound to be a layer that you will find hard to penetrate because that part of the individual is only known to them.

Case study: Judith Mawson was married to serial killer Gary Ridgeway and while living a perfectly normal happy married life with the man, had no reason to suspect that the man was a killer of 70 people. Thus, Gary Ridgeway was able to keep this core layer to himself, regardless of living with his wife for a period of 13 years.

Analyzing People to Uncover the Different Layers

When you learn how to analyze people and examine their different gestures and moves, this enables you to slowly uncover the different layers that make them. Through this, you are in a better position to understand people and make different decisions based on the information you find out about them. You can learn whether somebody is honest with you; whether or not a person is compatible with you; whether or not somebody is the right match for you and many other things. Valuable information about people helps you know why they act in a certain manner and enables you to discover what they think about you.

If profiling people interests you and you want to make the best use of this skill, then let us move on to the second chapter.

Case study of layers – In order for you to be convinced by our previous arguments, I have added a case study to show you how layers work. When Jennifer Wilson attended for an interview for a job, she looked nice on the outside, although her body language told the interviewers that she lacked confidence and was hiding something from them. Her "skin" layer gave bad body language, she fumbled and she looked downward when speaking to people. Her "second layer" revealed that many of the things that she liked didn't fit with other people within the workplace and thus made her a bad fit for the job. Her third layer became more apparent as the conversation went on and she proved herself to be someone who was more interested in income than doing a good job. In fact, she highlighted her self-importance in a few things that she said which gave the interviewers the clues that she was not suited to the job being offered. Of course, her core values were not apparent at the interview though would have become apparent had they hired her. These different layers of who we are count toward the way that people see us and had Jennifer worked on her interview skills, she may have made a better impression. She needed to do her homework, to find out more about the company, to present herself more articulately and to give the impression that she was more interested in the job that she was being interviewed for.

When you initially meet someone, you begin to peel back the layers to discover who that person is. This is something that you need to work on because you also need to understand that people also evaluate you in this way. In the following chapters, we will give you indications of what to look out for other than the initial layers of the onion because the human psyche is more complex than what you see on the surface or within those layers and much of what you learn about someone can be learned by recognizing micro expressions and the way that these portray what people are really thinking.

Chapter 2

Analyzing People through Their Sense of Style

When you meet new people, the first thing you are most likely to notice about them is their sense of style and how well or poorly they are dressed.

We all tend to have some sort of biasness towards people who have different dressing styles. For instance, we will tend to 'write off' someone who isn't nicely dressed and regard those who are nicely dressed highly. The type of clothes that someone is wearing also influences our view of them. For instance, we will tend to think differently when we meet someone in jeans compared to if we meet someone in a three-piece suit.

This clearly shows that your sense of style is a big factor that makes your personality.

Your Clothes Communicate to Others about You

Psychologists, Joanne Eicher and Marry Ellen Roach Higgins, carried a research study in 1992 on why people dress up in a certain manner. The study found out that one of the two main functions of clothes is to communicate to others.

This shows that your dress speaks volumes about your personality and traits to others. If you are a shy person, you will dress in a certain manner and if you are a bold, confident person, you will most likely wear clothes that are different from those worn by an introvert. Similarly, if you want to let someone know that you like them, you will dress pleasantly in front of them, but won't bother to put so much effort on yourself when you meet others. This proves that your dress says a lot about you.

Therefore, you need to take into consideration the way you and others dress when analyzing people.

Analyzing How People Dress Up

To better comprehend a person and to get a peek into their true nature, you need to look for the following signs in the way they dress up.

✓ **Casual Clothes that Hang Loosely**: If you see a person dressed up casually wearing clothes that hang loosely on them and are torn from several places, then it means that the person is nonchalant about the way they dress. They are probably quite messy and lack a sense of order in their life as well. However, if their clothes are neat, then it could mean they cannot afford to buy new and better clothes.

✓ **Expensive but Dirty Clothes**: People who wear expensive, gorgeous clothes that aren't properly cleaned aren't hygiene freaks. They care less about how perfect things are in their lives and are more concerned in enjoying their life.

✓ **Neat Clothes that are Properly Tucked in**: People who wear neat clothes that are properly tucked in and folded beautifully in the right places and are devoid of any creases regardless of the occasion they are dressed for are extremely organized, neat and decorous. They are most likely to be hygiene and control freaks and like things to be in a certain order. Actually, even an inch of inappropriate or unnecessary movement could disturb them. Additionally, they are strict about certain principles in their life and like living by their rules. Such people can be a little tough to deal with since they most likely have an obstinate nature.

✓ **Casual and Formal Clothes according to the Occasion**: People who dress up according to the occasion and wear casual or formal clothes that are neat and match the essence of an event are organized people who aren't too strict about rules and regulations in their lives. They like breaking free from norms frequently but aren't too wild either.

✓ **Rugged Clothes**: People who don't dress sharply all the time and are mostly found in rugged clothes have a free, wild and lively nature. They love breaking rules and living their life on their own terms and not on the norms dictated by the society.

✓ **Stylish and Polished Shoes**: If you see a person wearing clean, beautiful and shiny shoes, then it is quite likely that the person is extremely ambitious about their goals in life. They have particular lifelong goals they want to actualize and they have a plan to objectify these aims as well.

So, the next time you meet someone, look for these clues to analyze them better.

Observe their Hairstyle

You can as well consider someone's hairdo to learn more about them. For instance, if it is neatly brushed back or nicely cut, this signifies that they are organized people who live their life systematically.

On the other hand, people who hardly brush their hair or wear messy hairdos lack that order and system found in the lives of those discussed above. These people are carefree and aren't that opinionated either.

Additionally, people who are very particular about their hairdo and wear hairstyles that are in trend love fashion and want to abide by the latest trends and styles. Such people are fun to hang out with and you will mostly find them talking about fashion. So if you are a true fashionista and want to find people who share the same interest, then look for this sign in those around you by simply looking at their hair.

Examine their Hygiene

This is yet another way of analyzing people. Research shows that people who smell nice, look nice and have their nails and hair properly trimmed each time you meet them are extremely hygienic and prioritize cleanliness. Such people avoid messy places and rooms and keep their things in an orderly manner. Additionally, they have a certain routine they like to abide by and feel uneasy when they aren't able to follow it.

On the other hand, people who are untidy, give off body odor and have unclean hair don't have any routine in their life. Research also shows that such people are quite inconsiderate towards others and mostly care about themselves only. However, this isn't true for all messy and untidy people. Some people just don't pay much attention to themselves because they are lazy.

So the next time you want to find out what lies in the first layer of a person, you need to observe these indicators. But do not be fooled into thinking that appearance and style is everything. It is merely an indication and a first impression. Remember also that people may be judging you from the way that you present yourself and the style that you possess.

Chapter 3

Evaluating Their Talk

In addition to people's sense of style and hygiene, you should also analyze their character to know more about them. So how can you do that? Well, all you have to do is to analyze what they talk about and how they talk. Different studies show that the way people talk and the topics they discuss or are interested in have a lot to say about that person. Therefore, you must pay attention to these elements when you want to profile someone. Let us find out more about these.

The Things People Talk About

It is easy to understand a person's interests and likes based on the topics they talk about. For instance, if you meet someone who is constantly blabbering about animals and documentaries on animals, then you can easily conclude that the person is an animal lover. Similarly, if a person always brings up the topic of religion or women empowerment each time you sit down to have a chat with them, then it shows that the person cares about that particular topic only and that subject governs their entire life.

However, if you meet someone who loves gossiping and cannot find a better activity than that, then you need to stay away from that person. It is obvious that the person loves discussing others so they are most likely going to discuss something about you with others as well. Since all gossips aren't always true and that person is aware of this fact, you can conclude that the person is dishonest as well. People who enjoy gossiping often are quite likely to spread rumors about others for the sake of fun and find no harm in destroying other people's reputation. Such people can be dangerous so it is best to avoid them. However, this doesn't mean that all people who gossip are bad. Gossiping occasionally is alright, but making it a habit is where you cross the line.

Masculine and Feminine Topics

Moreover, you can analyze a person based on the nature of topics they talk about. If you find a person taking interest in feminine or masculine topics particularly, then it means they are trying to tap into their feminine or masculine sides, respectively. For instance, if you see a girl hanging out with guys her age mostly and taking interest in sports, archery and hunting, then it shows that she likes her masculine side and isn't interested in her femininity that much. Also, it could mean that she isn't insecure about her femininity and is strong enough to dig deeper into her masculine side.

This can be supported by a real life example. M. Farouk Radwan is a psychologist who runs the website, 2knowmyself, and analyzes people. While talking about one of his clients 'Sarah', he said that he found out a lot about her personality through the topics she talked about. He saw her taking great interest in topics related to guys that showed that she wasn't that pleased with her feminine side. Later, he found out that this was so because Sarah was raised in a family where men were glorified and women were degraded. This means that your childhood or upbringing has a lot to do with whether you are attracted to masculine or feminine topics. The next time you come across a guy who is fascinated by fashion and is more interested in feminine subjects, this may mean that he was brought up in a family with more women than men.

Tone

Apart from concentrating on what topics people talk about when engaging in various discussions, you should also pay some attention to their tone. Look at the following indicators that you need to notice in a person's voice to help you get more insight into their character.

- **Soft Tone**: If a person has a soft tone and talks to others in a gentle voice, this is probably an indicator of their introvert personality. People who talk to others in a feeble tone are most likely to be shy and find it difficult to boldly talk to others.

- **Monotonous Tone**: If the person you are conversing with speaks in a monotonous tone, then it shows that they are bored. They aren't interested in what you have to talk about and wouldn't mind ending it. If you find them talking with everyone else in the same manner, this may be an indication that the person has an indifferent character and is probably not interested in anyone else. This may also mean that they tend to have a high opinion about themselves. Geraldine Barkworth is a speech therapist and director at the Goddess of Public Speaking in Australia. She too validates this point and stated that many of her clients with a monotonous tone do not pay attention to what people around them are saying and consult her to add more color to their tone, so they can hide their lack of interest when talking to uninteresting people.

- **Change in Tone**: If somebody's tone changes when defending their opinion or their tone is generally loud, but shifts to a softer version when talking to a domineering person, then this shift reflects their lack of confidence. That person isn't self-assured and probably finds trouble in expressing their opinion in front of others.

- **Extremely Loud Tone**: People who tend to talk in a loud voice are confident, extrovert and have a bad habit of speaking in a brash tone. This habit also represents how they were raised as a child. Either everyone around them had a loud tone, or they formed a poor habit and their parents never corrected it.

- **Excited Tone**: If a person talks in an excited tone most of the time, then it means they enjoy the little pleasures of life and are mostly easy to please.

- **Shrill and High Tone**: People with a very sharp and high tone are often ignored by the important people in their lives and aren't authoritative, which is why they use a high voice as a coping mechanism to hide their insecurities.

- **Strong, Authoritative, and Deep Tone**: According to Geraldine, most of her clients exhibiting these characteristics in their tone have good leadership skills and are extremely confident.

You need to lookout for these indicators to understand those around you.

Words Used by a Person

Another significant symbol of a person's character is the words they frequently use in their speech. If you find using abusive language/words frequently, then it means several things.

- ✓ For starters, they could have a casual personality and don't like being formal in their talk.
- ✓ Secondly, they could have an immoral character and lack the ethics required to speak modestly to others.
- ✓ Thirdly, it could mean that they suffered through a severe episode in their life and have been seriously wounded deep inside. The harsh words they use are

to express their anger as they make them feel a little light inside.

People who are eloquent in their speech and use soft words while conversing with others have a polished personality. It is probable that they are extremely refined and know their moral values. However, in some cases, it is a sign of a hypocrite nature. Some clever and tactful people use their eloquence to hide their true identity and insensitive personality.

As you can see from the above explanations, the style of talking and subjects discussed by people reveal different traits about their personality, which is why you must closely examine these factors when analyzing people.

Case study: Evaluating talk – In an interview with a potential client, I was surprised at the level of their knowledge on subjects not usually associated with their sex. In this particular interview, the client talked about the efficiency of the motor in a specific Japanese car. She was well dressed and articulate and had made the effort to look nice for the interview. What surprised me was the language that she used once the ice was broken between us. However, you also need to take into account the background of the person to whom you are speaking. In this particular case, she used what may be described as colorful language but clearly did not lack ethics. She also gave the impression that she was able to converse at a very high technological level so I had no question about her professionalism. Therefore, I assumed that she was of the first type mentioned in the above resume – in that she enjoyed the lack of formality in her speech.

This was backed up by the fact that she was mixing in social circles where this kind of language would be commonplace and working with male counterparts on a regular basis. Her tone was an excited tone which showed me that she was enthusiastic about her work life. In fact, at times her tone was deep which gave her the appearance of knowing what she was talking about. I was right on all points and was able to understand and read her way of thinking instantly once I had eliminated all other possibilities. She was a woman in a man's world and had adapted her way of speaking to fit into what was normal in that particular case.

Chapter 4

Reading Their Body Language

So far, you have learned about different aspects that can help make it easy for you to decode people's behaviors and character with ease. We will now move to another aspect of understanding people, body language. Professional therapists and FBI profilers use body language to examine people all the time.

The way you position your hands, arms, legs, torso, head, and eyes speaks volumes of different things about your personality and the things going on in your head. Let us find out the different body language cues you can use for analyzing people.

Eye Contact

According to body language experts, seasoned therapists and FBI profilers, your eyes greatly represent what you are thinking and your personality, so you need to look at the eye movements of people you're trying to analyze. Here are a few things you need to look out for:

- **Moving Eyes to the Right**: Moving your eyeball towards the right signifies that you are hiding something. However, it is normal when you are telling stories or thinking of creative plans. So when people constantly look towards the right when talking, then it is likely that they are fabricating the truth.

- **Moving Eyes to the Left**: When you look towards your left, you are usually trying to recall some information as your brain's left side is responsible for storing facts, information and memories. Therefore, when you see someone moving their eyes towards the left when you ask them an important question, then it means they are trying to remember the answer to your query.

- **Direct Eye Contact**: If someone is maintaining direct eye contact, this could mean 2 things: either they are incredibly confident, or they are lying to you.

Keep these clues in mind when talking to people so you can easily spot if they are lying to you.

Mouth Movements and Smile

Your mouth movements and smile tell different things about your character too. Therefore, it is important that you observe these elements in a person when you attempt to study them.

- **Pasted Smile**: If you see someone flashing a pasted smile at you, this probably means that they feel they have better things to do than to waste their time talking to you.

- **Clenching Lips when Smiling**: Clenching lips when smiling is usually an indicator that the person you're talking to is either hiding something or is frustrated by your talk.

- **Dropping Jaws when Smiling**: People are quite likely to drop their jaws in two situations. For starters, they are likely to do that when they are truly amazed or shocked by new information. Secondly, they do that when trying to fake their smile and interest in your talk. To figure out if someone is faking a smile and isn't really amazed, you should see the look in their eyes. If their eyes appear as shocked as the smile on their face, this means that their smile is genuine and they are startled. On the other hand, if the eyes don't seem to reflect what the face is showing, this means that they are faking it.

- **Bottom Lip hanging Out**: If you see a person jutting out their lower lip, this probably means that they are upset with about an issue and are probably looking for a sympathetic shoulder to cry on.

- **Biting, Chewing and Grinding Actions**: People bite and chew their lips and grind their teeth when they are anxious, stressed, and depressed. So when you find someone doing any of these actions, it is probably due to the stress they are undergoing.

As you can see, there's a meaning behind each of your facial and mouth movements. Therefore, you need to watch out for all these if you really want to know more about someone.

Head Movements

You tend to move your head in a certain way when experiencing different emotions. This simply means that this part of your body can help you know a lot about a person. Let's take a quick look at a few head movements to help you analyze people better.

- **Nodding the Head**: When people nod their head while talking to you, it means they agree with you. However, if they tend to move their head sideways and move their eyes to the right while nodding their head, it means that they are concealing their true emotions and don't really agree with you.

- **Holding Head Upwards and High and jutting the Chin**: If someone has their head held upwards and high while jutting their chin, this is likely to mean that they think high of themselves or are big headed; of course unless they have a neck fracture.

- **Tilting the Head**: When a person keeps their head tilted while talking to you, it may mean two things. For starters, it may mean that they trust you. It may also mean that they are analyzing you and probably sizing you up. If one of their eyebrows is slightly raised or they have a stiff expression on their face, this probably means they are analyzing you and sizing you up.

- **Keeping the Head Down**: If a person keeps their head down when talking to you, there is a high likelihood that they don't agree with you but are trying to hide their disapproval.

- **Shaking the Head**: Shaking the head sideways means a person is frustrated and is trying to conceal that feeling, and if they constantly shake their head forcefully, it shows that they don't approve of your opinion.

Considering these head movements while observing someone will certainly give you more insight into their personality.

Arm and Hand Movements

You can also use arm and hand movements to analyze people. So what is it that you should be looking out for? Here is what to look out for to analyze people:

- **Self-hugging**: Self-hugging or folding arms when talking to someone is often referred to as a gesture of reluctance. If you observe someone using this gesture when talking to you, this may mean that they don't want to talk to you.
- **Clenching Fists while Crossing Arms**: If someone crosses their arms and clenches their fists simultaneously, there is a high likelihood that they are showing their stubbornness and anger towards you or the person they are talking to.

- **Holding Your Arm Behind Your Body**: Keeping your hands tied back together while clasping your hands is a sign of confidence. So, if you see a person exhibiting this gesture, it means they are brimming with confidence and have a high self-worth.

- **Scratching the Shoulder by Holding Your Arm across Your Body**: When someone uses this gesture, it may mean that they are nervous and anxious.

- **Keeping Your Hand on the Heart**: Placing your hand right on your heart's location is a gesture to show your honesty. When somebody makes this body language movement, they probably want you to believe what they are saying.

- **Touching Your Fingertips with Your Thumb**: Although people often use this gesture when doing yoga or meditation, they can also use it to mean that they contemplate a lot and are mindful of everything around them. Such people are extremely alert, focused, poised, and calm. In addition, they know what's going on around them so you need to be careful and tactful around them. They are also not the kind of people who you can fool easily.

- **Cracking the Knuckles**: If you see someone cracking their knuckles, then it means they are going through some pressure and are trying to calm themselves down. It may also mean that someone wants to attract your attention.
- **Touching the Nose when Speaking**: This is a classic sign that someone is lying.
- **Stroking the Chin Using Your Hand**: When you see someone doing this gesture, it means they are in a thoughtful mode and are deeply pondering on an issue.
- **Keeping Your Hands on your Hips**: The akimbo position is a sign of confidence. So if someone does that, it means that they have high confidence levels.
- **Placing Hands in Pockets**: When you see someone performing this gesture, then it means that person is bored and is feeling lazy.

You've definitely learnt a lot about body language so far. From now on, make sure to remember these clues so you can make the most of them when you are in a mood to study people.

Movements of Your Torso

The torso can convey important messages about your mood too so you need to analyze the torso of the people you are trying to analyze. For instance, if you see someone angling their torso and maintaining a certain distance from you or the one they are conversing with, it means they are angry with you or that person. Similarly, if they keep their torso straight and move forward towards you, then it is because they are pleased with you and want to come closer to you. These cues can be particularly helpful for you when you want to analyze your partner's mood.

Feet and Leg Movements

Your body language is incomplete without the movements shown by your feet and legs in different situations. Therefore, this is another factor you must be attentive to when examining somebody in detail. Here are some important things you need to look out for when studying a person's feet and leg movements.

- **Pointing Knees towards someone when sitting**: If a person is sitting and has their knees unintentionally pointed towards you, then it is possibly because they are strongly engrossed in your speech and are mesmerized by you. It may also mean that someone is attracted to you.

- **Locking the Ankles**: If you see someone locking both their ankles when sitting, it means they are trying to suppress their negative emotions.

- **Crossing the Legs**: If a person is standing with their legs slightly crossed, then this gesture probably indicates their lack of self-confidence. By spotting this gesture, you can easily differentiate between the confident and unconfident people.

- **Shoe Play**: When you see a woman doing shoe play and looking keenly at a man, it means she's deeply interested in him. By identifying this gesture, you can find out whether or not a girl in your group of friends is sexually attracted towards any of your friends or you.

- **Unintentionally Pointing Your Foot Towards a Person**: If you observe a person unintentionally pointing their foot towards another person, it means that they are pointing towards the dominating person.

Now that we've covered many of the things that relate to body language, let us now learn other aspects of analyzing people that can make things easier for you as you analyze people.

Case study – Body language – Looking at the body language of speakers in a recent conference, one particular speaker stood out from the crowd for all of the wrong reasons. His stance was wrong. He looked down and thus his voice did not carry sufficiently for people to understand fully what was being said. His posture was lazy and playing with his hands said that he lacked confidence. Upon interviewing him after the conference, it turned out that he had been singled out at the last minute to replace a speaker who could not make the event. He was incompetent at what he was asked to do and the impression gained by the audience was that the man needed to be in another job!

If you want to put yourself over as an authority or have yourself taken seriously, you need to be able to work on your body language. This is the main thing that people will judge you on, when other criteria is not available to them – such as in the case of meeting strangers. Since no one knew the background of this speaker, they could only judge him on his performance which was disappointing at best – both for him and for the audience that had to sit through his narration. However, empathy upon getting to know the speaker was easy because being placed in that situation was embarrassing for him as well as for you. Empathy will serve you helpings of common sense when it comes to getting to know people and you will see in future chapters how to use this in your reading of others to get over initial instincts and get beyond them to understand who the real person is.

Chapter 5

More Helpful Clues for Analyzing People

So far, we have discussed numerous important elements and signs that can help you profile people effectively. Let us throw light on a few more clues that can help you master this skill.

Respect for Time

How people value their time and that of others speaks greatly of how responsible they are. For instance, if someone is keen on managing their time such that they keep time whenever you agree to meet, this is a clear sign that the person is highly punctual and values their time. They do not like squandering time and are probably great time managers. They know the value of time and are able to make the best use of it. Also, it is quite likely that they are highly determined to accomplish their goals in life.

On the other hand, if you see someone idling around and not using their time productively, then it is a sign of their lazy, carefree, and irresponsible nature. They might have big goals and dreams, but they lack the necessary will and motivation to actualize them. Such people will tend to have big plans one day and feel hopeless the next day just because they feel they have no control over their life.

Regularity

If you see someone visiting a certain place at a certain time daily, it means they are regular, punctual, and organized. For instance, if they have a tendency of going to the gym at the same time every single day, this is indication that they are highly resolute about achieving their goals in life.

Being regular with certain important activities also shows your area of interest. For instance, if you see someone going to the gym daily, this may mean that they truly like spending time at the gym.

Hurried Behavior

The hurried and rushed behavior of those around you is another factor that can help you analyze them better. For example, if someone exhibits a disturbed behavior and is always in a hurry to do things, this probably means that they are bad at time management. They don't know what tasks to prioritize and what to let go of, which is why they rush through different chores to complete them on time. Additionally, it could also mean that they lack focus and become easily distracted. People whose attention easily becomes scattered tend to hurry through every task and often leave one incomplete to pursue another.

Keeping the Plate Full

Do you know of someone who loves keeping their plate full at all times? Well, if you do, then this signifies that the person is trying too hard to be a perfectionist. People who chase perfectionism often become involved in multiple activities at the same time. Obviously, you can only do this for so long. You will soon feel overwhelmed.

Temper

You can also consider the manner in which someone can manage their temper when analyzing them. For instance, if someone is so short-tempered that they cannot control their rage in even simple, uncomplicated situations, such a person is likely to have a volatile personality. Short-tempered people are most likely to have a dynamic personality and aren't good at managing stress. They are also likely to have chronic anger problems and won't be composed. Their short temper could be a sign of their lack of confidence, inability to fulfill their goals and their impatience.

On the other hand, if someone is collected, calm and composed, they are likely to have deep insight into their true identity. This is especially because they have been successful at controlling their emotions and know how to express emotions the best way. Such people are great to hang out with as they are likely to influence you positively.

Optimism and Pessimism

Another factor you can use to analyze people is how they perceive their life and everything around them. Are they optimistic about life in general or do they have a pessimistic attitude?

People who are positive and hopeful radiate positivity. Such people will always appear cheerful or at least hopeful even in the toughest situations and will always have something deep and meaningful to say. To identify such people, you should look at their expressions in time of tension. If you find them becoming calm after a few moments of silence and worry, then yes, they are positive.

However, if their concern seems to aggravate with time, this is a sign that they are more pessimistic. Pessimistic people mostly have a worried look on their face and become hopeless even when there is a slight change in how they desire things to be. Such people are unconfident and unrealistic, and tend to make you lose hope as well.

Case study – cup half full and cup half empty

In this study, we can pretty well tell the kind of person we are dealing with by watching out for signals in their behavior which are negative or positive. When James Elliot was given six complete strangers to interview, he had to decide which were suitable for a given project. The project needed a lot of dynamism and he knew that unless the positivity was there, it would not be completed on time. The first thing that he looked for was negativity and three of the applicants showed this during their conversation. He marked down positive responses and negative responses.

Over the course of the interviews, his notes told him exactly which people were suited to the project although there was a tie between two particular candidates who he met on an informal basis in order to make his decision. From that short casual conversation over a cup of coffee he was able to see through the façade of one of the applicants by seeing their negative side and was able to choose applicants whose enthusiasm and belief in the project would get it done. He was right in his choices since they all saw the cup as half full rather than half empty and it was this enthusiasm for life and positivity that got the job finalized. By showing your positive side to people, you gain more approval than by showing your negative side and make yourself more easily read by someone who is looking for openness.

Chapter 6

Intuition

Human intuition plays a vital part in reading people. We have covered the obvious things such as the way that people dress and present themselves. We have also covered body language, but bearing all of these attributes in mind, there is a card left up your sleeve that will help you to read people and that is your own intuition. If your intuition tells you that something is wrong, it generally is.

Intuitive empathy is a tool that you can use in your favor. If you feel for the person that you are listening to but he/she doesn't fit the criteria of person that you thought you were seeking for a particular position in your company, your intuitive empathy may help out.

Case study – Intuitive empathy – In 1968, I was asked to interview 30 women for three positions within the company. There were many criteria to take into account.

The applicant had to be reasonably well presented as the company needed someone who was a fairly good flagship for the company's reputation. A strict dress code was imposed, so that helped to single out those that had not even passed this for their interview.

The other items that they needed to get through were a spelling test of some level of difficulty relevant to the job and an explanation of why they wanted the job. I had singled down two people and had the last one to decide upon but was a little indecisive about my reading of the applicants and didn't want to make a wrong decision for the last position available. However, my gut instinct kept taking me back to one applicant who – on the surface – seemed unsuitable. She dressed correctly, she answered the questions, her spelling was not the best but there was something about her that brought out intuitive empathy. She had tried harder to find work than any other applicant had. In fact, the others – in comparison with her – were apathetic in their approach. I was able to read that this woman needed the job and would therefore be unlikely to up and leave as so many others had in the past. She was suited to certain tasks that others did not particularly like and there was a certain amount of work that could be given to her that didn't require good spelling skills.

Asked in for a second interview – my gut instinct still told me that she had more going for her than the other applicants. She was desperate to get a job and had not spent the whole summer after leaving school simply lounging around on a beach. She was earnest in her approach and would have been very servile which suited the job position which was available.

Based on common sense, she would not have been considered. She failed in the tests and should have been turned down. However, my empathy toward this particular interviewee was proven to be perfectly justified and she is still in that job now and still excelling at it because she was so grateful to be given a chance.

If you do feel intuitive empathy toward someone, this is a good sign that the person is indeed the right person for what you have to offer them, even if that is merely friendship. This reading of a person using your intuitive empathy is a very effective way of getting to trust your gut instinct and making accurate diagnosis of whether the person will work out to be the person you suspected them to be.

Often people have their own biases. They may not, for example, like to make friends with those who do not look nice. They may mix in cliques of people who are of a similar background or type. However, once in a while you can see relationships form where intuitive empathy has been used to override the normal criteria used to judge someone and where dissimilar people get along quite nicely. You may find unlikely friends in your lifetime. These will be people who have understood each other and who have developed friendships, not based upon similar style or background, but based upon similar standards and morals. These could turn out to be the best of friends because their friendship isn't based on the superficial. Thus, do not dismiss people simply based upon their outward appearance. There may be more to them than you at first suspected and you will only get to know that as you begin to peel away the layers of the "onion" that hide who they are.

Chapter 7

Using the Right Cues and Looking for Responses

The FBI interview thousands of different people and during their interviews have to make decisions which may result in incarceration. They may also result in gaining information though people are not always honest when answering FBI agents and thus, they have developed different ways of being able to read the people that they are interviewing.

Looking for clues in the words chosen

When talking to someone, they may look out for clues that lead them to the conclusion that someone is an egoist. This may be someone who enjoys bragging about their achievements and making a big deal about them. They may also exaggerate the truth. A phrase such as "I won an award" would become "I won another award" and this gives the indication that the person being spoken to wants you to know that his/her award winning was not confined to one event. How does this help? It helps in establishing whether the person being interviewed has their own agenda or will skew the truth to show the good side of his/her character, rather than being straightforward.

Recognizing signs of stress

Stress indicates that someone has been made uncomfortable by the question that has been asked. Thus, it's very useful to note stress while talking to someone.

Case study: When Sergeant Wally Travis interviewed a potential perpetrator, he kept noticing that the perp would tighten the jaw line when questions were asked that he was uncomfortable with answering. His stress was obvious. Other signs exist, but each individual that you deal with will show different signs. Look for the stress points because this may indicate that someone is not being honest.

The heart rate may also fluctuate when you are talking to someone and clearly feeling that the conversation is stressful.

Case study: Tony Bailey explained that when he was interviewing someone after a fire had been caused at a school, something that he noticed was that one particular child kept reaching for his throat while he was being interviewed. He suspected that this motion was for a specific reason and it seems that when people do this, they are trying to keep their heart rate under control because they know that what they are saying is untrue. Watch out for this gesture as it may just stop you from believing something erroneous.

There are many signs that someone is telling you lies or that your questions are causing them discomfort and you need to observe people to recognize them. For example, look at yourself in the mirror and ask yourself a question you know would embarrass you and look at your facial expression to see what it does. It's an instinct and immediate response to being made to feel uncomfortable. Observe in people. You may get friends and family to participate. Explain about your study and ask a series of questions that will occasionally change to a type of question that you know they may feel stressed about answering as this gives you a lot of clues about how people react.

They may simply react by being defensive, although you need to keep a close eye on what their hands are doing, movements of their eyes and the kind of body language that is coming from them. These all gives clues. Imagine what is going on inside of someone when they experience a sudden rise in blood pressure and it is this kind of discomfort that is translated on the outside that you will learn to recognize instantly.

Look out for bravado because often this hides an insecure interior. People joke because they are afraid of people actually getting to know who hides behind the façade. Similarly, loud people may be very quiet inside and not let anyone get near enough to them to know who they really are. These may appear to be authoritative, when in fact, they have little authority and must voice their opinions in a loud manner because they believe this makes up for their lack of stature.

Chapter 8

Understanding Micro Expressions

To communicate well and to gain the most from your reading of other people you need to understand something which is called micro expressions. These are expressions which help you to read people in a more efficient manner and are split into three types:

- Masked
- False
- Micro

A masked expression is when someone uses a facial expression to cover up their real feelings or when they know that they have made a micro expression and don't want you to read it. A case in point would be when you are interviewing someone and ask their opinion on a particular subject. They don't know whether you approve or not and may take your question lightly.

You: How do you feel about gun ownership?

The first expression is the one that is natural and may only last a couple of seconds and they may approve of gun ownership. However, when they see the stern expression on your face, they may mask that expression so that you think that their response is different. These are easy to notice if you remain observant all the time that you are talking to someone. A simple change of expression may be put on to mask their true feelings and this is very helpful in determining how truthful someone is being with you.

The false expression is one that is intentional. The person that you are talking to is telling you a lie and in order to make you believe that lie, their expression will be accompanied by body language which may give that lie away. Their face may be telling you one thing while their body language may be telling you something entirely different.

A micro expression is something that you see on someone's face before they react in a conversational manner. They may not know that you have noticed it but it's a good indication of what their response is to the conversation in question.

Emotional intelligence and empathy are improved by noticing these expressions. For example, in the case where I was interviewing different women for a job, I picked up on the expression on the face of the under-qualified applicant who eventually got the job. She got that job based on my empathetic feeling that she was the right person for the job – regardless of what the documentation said and her micro expression was what made me make that decision. It was one of earnestness and total honesty and my intuition was able to pick up on that.

If you want to get a long way in your career, it's important that you practice picking up on micro expressions. It helps you to understand others and to make great friendships but it does more than that. It also helps you to read what it is that they are saying, even if the words are unspoken and simple read between the spoken words. You are able to more efficiently spot those people who are telling you lies and are thus able to distinguish these from those who are giving truthful answers. When studies were done on micro expressions, what was found was that people who were able to read them made more popular coworkers and were thus able to mix with all kinds of people and get a favorable response from their relationships.

The other thing that noticeably increases is your own ability to desist from using negative micro expressions when you are talking to others because you become conscious of what they do to your credibility and are able to have a much more honest approach. This helps in the workplace and it also helps with personal relationships where you may have, in the past, sent out the wrong signals.

Although there are many courses available on understanding micro expressions, you also need to understand that the more you exercise observation of other people, the more you are able to learn about these on your own. This translates in your mind to being able to gage your own signals so that people are reading you in the way that you want them to. You are also able to hide those expressions that you may well have shown on your face before you understood how easily people read micro expressions. Thus, any understanding you gain from observation will help you to develop who you are and how you present yourself to others.

A typical TV commercial that demonstrates micro expressions is one where a couple are planning to take a vacation. As soon as the wife realizes that health cover is not an issue, she immediately thinks of inviting her mother. The micro expression on her husband's face is one of disapproval but he quickly turns that around once he realizes how important it is to his wife that her mother goes with them.

When one rolls one's eyes at an idea that has been suggested, this is a micro expression that leaves absolutely no room for maneuver because it's obvious that the person who makes this expression – even if followed up by an approving smile – that disapproval has already been demonstrated.

The reactions that people give you in an instance are often more honest than those they give you in retrospect. Thus, you need to look people in the eye when you are talking to them, in able to decipher from their actions whether that person is being totally honest with you. You may also determine what they really think about something from that micro expression and that's helpful in reading someone.

Case study: When James Willis was asked on stage for his opinion of the Royal Family, he was being filmed. This was for a documentary. Unfortunately, his micro expression gave him away totally when he gave the interviewer a sheepish grin that showed that he had no feeling whatsoever for the Royal Family and that he was sick of hearing about them. He was quick to mask this expression, though viewers will have picked up on it straight away.

Watching TV can actually help you to understand micro expressions better because you can see people talking while they are facing you and interviews are particularly good for picking up messages which are not spoken about simply by observing the expressions on the face of those who are in discussion.

Conclusion

With everything we've learnt so far, you shouldn't have a problem when analyzing people to know whatever it is you want to know about them. However, you can only make the best use of it if you put into practice what you have learnt. With constant practice, you will certainly become good at profiling people and will see what a positive impact it can have on your life.

The reason that this impact is so positive is because you also understand how people see you and what difference it can make to their opinion of you if your body language or your micro language is giving them all the wrong answers. You learn to communicate in a better way and will make more friends. You will be more popular in the workplace and are likely to be singled out for promotion, based on the fact that your astute nature will be recognized for what it is.

Those who understand how to read people are also better equipped to use the right people for the right tasks. They make great team leaders and in the workplace can only benefit the employer. They get through interviews with flying colors and know what to expect of interviewers from that first glance at them, being able to read into their expressions what it is that they seek.

They are also more conscious of how they present themselves and will have values that they know cannot be questioned. The other thing is that the better you become at reading people, the better you are able to trust your instincts and your gut feelings about people. You will feel intuitive empathy toward the right people and won't waste your time empathizing with those who have no intention of being helpful. You will recognize qualities in people and be able to produce that quality in yourself.

Every once in a while someone will come into your life that will surprise you and when they do, try to learn something from them. How did they do it? What were the signs? These are people who are very good at hiding the real self and they may even have a reason for doing so. Their reasons may be honorable or they may be dishonest. As the murderer's wife said, no one was more shocked than she at the horror of her husband's crimes. However, when you do come across someone that you misread and who you subsequently find to intelligent and fun, you can learn a lot from them because they are classic examples of people who know the importance of communication and who have mastered the skills of communication to such an extent that they can still keep their cards hidden up their sleeve, to bring out when it suits them and that's where you need to be headed. When you get there, it's a wonderful place to be where opportunity lies in every corner and you can be sure that you will be there to grab it with both hands, able to communicate with the people you need to propel you forward in your career.

The better you are able to read people, the better you are able to communicate yourself and what you have learned within the pages of this book should help you to improve your communication skills and learn to use them in an honest and straightforward way that helps you to work out the route that will take you to the future – knowing that whatever event arises, you are ready to take on the challenge of being able to analyze and use that analysis to equip you for the years to come.